The Hungarian Revolution, 1956

Rupert Colley

Copyright © 2016 Rupert Colley
CreateSpace Edition

All rights reserved.
ISBN: 978-1537553825
1537553828

Rupert Colley was born one Christmas Day and grew up in Devon. A history graduate, he worked as a librarian in London before starting 'History In An Hour' – a series of non-fiction history ebooks that can be read in just sixty minutes, acquired by Harper Collins in 2011. He has also penned eight works of historical fiction. Now a full time writer, speaker and the author of historical novels, he lives in Waltham Forest, London with his wife, two children and dog.

Works by Rupert Colley:

Fiction:
My Brother the Enemy
The Black Maria
The Sixth Man
The Torn Flag
The Unforgiving Sea
The White Venus
The Woman on the Train
This Time Tomorrow

History In An Hour series:
1914: History In An Hour
Black History: History In An Hour
D-Day: History In An Hour
Hitler: History In An Hour
Mussolini: History In An Hour
Nazi Germany: History In An Hour
Stalin: History In An Hour
The Afghan Wars: History In An Hour
The Cold War: History In An Hour
The Russian Revolution: History In An Hour
The Siege of Leningrad: History In An Hour
World War One: History In An Hour
World War Two: History In An Hour

Other non-fiction:
The Savage Years: Tales From the 20th Century
The Battle of the Somme
A History of the World Cup: An Introduction

The Hungarian Revolution, 1956

Historyinanhour.com
Rupertcolley.com

'October 23, 1956, is a day that will live forever in the annals of free men and nations. It was a day of courage, conscience and triumph. No other day since history began has shown more clearly the eternal unquenchability of man's desire to be free, whatever the odds against success, whatever the sacrifice required.'

John F. Kennedy

Table of Contents

Introduction	1
Hungary, 1914 to 1919	3
The Horthy Years	12
Post-War	27
Post-Stalin	45
Uprising	58
Post-1956	86
Blood in the Water	90
1989	96
The Torn Flag	103
Other works by Rupert Colley	109

Introduction

On 22 October 1956, a large group of students gathered in a Budapest university hall and, after much discussion, drew-up a 16-point manifesto. Amongst other demands, they called for freedom of speech and freedom of expression; they called for open, multi-party elections and the removal of Soviet troops from Hungarian soil. It was, in the context of the time, an incredibly brave and daring undertaking. The following day, they posted-up copies of their manifesto on trees and lampposts across the city before starting out on a march. Thousands joined the procession, gathering in front of the parliament building, shouting their demands. Without really having planned it, the students of Budapest had unleashed an uprising that quickly spread across the capital and the whole country.

The Hungarian Revolution of 1956 constituted the most serious threat to Soviet hegemony throughout the Cold War years. It was ultimately unsuccessful. Anger and the justice of the cause can only take you so far when faced with the might of a professional, organised army.

But 33 years' later, with the memories of the uprising still fresh in the mind, it spurred-on those who sought once again to end communist rule in Hungary. One by one, the communist regimes fell throughout Eastern Europe during 1989, including Hungary's. Finally, after 40 years of totalitarian rule, Hungary was free.

Hungary, 1914 to 1919

Hungary had been part of the Austro-Hungarian empire, the 'Dual Monarchy', since 1867, ruled by the House of Habsburg, in the person of Franz Joseph. The empire consisted of several nationalities, who, on occasions, sought greater autonomy. The empire resisted all such calls – for fear even the smallest of concessions would only lead to demands for more. Indeed, in the Hungarian half of the empire, its rulers enforced a policy of 'Magyarization', an attempt to make its people more 'Hungarian'. Amongst the many nationalities causing the empire difficulty were the Serbs of Bosnia who wished to be incorporated into the nation of Serbia. On 28 June 1914, in Sarajevo, a Bosnian Serb called Gavrilo Princip assassinated the heir to the Austro-Hungarian throne, Franz Ferdinand. The assassination proved to be the spark that rapidly led to war.

Franz Joseph, c1905.

Franz Joseph died, aged 86, on 21 November 1916. He was succeeded by his grand-nephew,

Charles, who became Charles I of Austria and Charles IV of Hungary, the last emperor of Austria and the last king of Hungary.

The war was going badly for the Austro-Hungarians. On 7 December 1917, the United States declared war on Austria-Hungary and in June 1918, it lost to Italy in the Battle of Piave.

On 31 October, socialist Mihály Károlyi, with the support of the Hungarian army, staged a coup in Budapest and took power in what became known as the 'Aster Revolution', on account of the aster flowers they wore in their hats. The coup caused the collapse of the Habsburg Empire. Charles IV bowed to the inevitable and the 'Hungarian Democratic Republic' was proclaimed on 16 November 1918 with Károlyi its president.

On 11 November, the Western Front armistice came into effect. The First World War was over.

A year before, in November 1917, the Bolsheviks, led by the charismatic Vladimir Lenin, had seized power in Russia. In Hungary, a left-wing soldier fighting in the Austro-Hungarian army, named Bela Kun, was taken prisoner by the Russians. While in captivity, inspired by the Bolshevik revolution, Kun became a dedicated communist. On release, he met Lenin, learnt Russian and fought for the Bolsheviks during the Russian Civil War (1917 – 1922). In late 1918, armed with Russian money, supplies and men, Kun returned to Budapest and founded the Hungarian Communist Party.

Meanwhile, Károlyi's government was struggling. Severe inflation, mass unemployment and food shortages undermined his authority and resulted in widespread protests, much of which was organised by Kun's communists, although Kun himself had been imprisoned. On 21 March 1919, after only four months in power, Károlyi resigned.

Bela Kun and his communists, in coalition with the Social Democrats, formed a government and established the 'Hungarian Soviet Republic', the first Soviet power outside Russia. Lenin, although pleased at this development, was still appalled that Hungary's communists had had to compromise with the Social Democrats.

Bela Kun, c1923.

Kun was certainly radical – he nationalised industry, banks, the press and much private property; and declared his intention to collectivize the land, angering the peasantry, his main supporters, who had anticipated he would give them the land. Kun again undermined his rural support when he tried to requisition food for the cities.

Meanwhile, following the war, the victorious nations met at the Paris Peace Conference, starting 19 January 1919, to decide the fates of the vanquished nations. Proceedings were dominated by the 'Big Four': US president, Woodrow Wilson; British prime minister, David Lloyd George; French prime minister, Georges Clemenceau; and Italian prime minister, Vittorio Orlando. The conference produced five peace treaties – one for each of the defeated nations. The Treaty of Trianon devastated Hungary. Ruthenia and Slovakia went to the newly-created state of Czechoslovakia, Croatia went to Yugoslavia, another newly-created state, and the province of Transylvania (consisting of 1.5 million Magyars) to Romania. Post-war Hungary was now just 28 per cent the size of pre-war Hungary and had become a landlocked nation; and its population only 36 per cent the pre-war population. Half of Hungary's ten largest pre-war cities were allocated to other countries. 3.4 million Magyars (over a third) now lived outside Hungary. The Hungarians were not invited to discuss the terms of the treaty and had no option but to sign.

Although the Treaty of Trianon was not signed and ratified until 4 June 1920, its proposed contents were known a year before. Hence in May 1919, Bela Hun tried to restore Hungary's pre-war boundaries by invading Slovakia, that was now part of Czechoslovakia, and Romania. The invasion in Slovakia was briefly successful in that, under Kun's direction, they were able to establish a Soviet Republic in southeast Slovakia. But it was short-lived – existing only a matter of weeks, from 16 June to 7 July 1919. Kun's expedition into Romania, to try and recapture Transylvania, was equally unsuccessful.

On 24 June, in light of these failures, and with the economy spiralling out of control, Hungary's Social Democrats tried to oust the communists from power. They failed. Kun responded with terror. Those suspected of having been involved in the attempted coup were executed. Groups of men, the 'Lenin Boys', were dispatched to terrorize the population, intimidate and murder. One Lenin Boy leader urged his men forward, exclaiming, 'suffocate them in their own blood! Beat their heads wherever you find them!' Vladimir Lenin, himself, encouraged his Hungarian comrades to 'shoot them'. Hungary's period of 'Red Terror' had begun.

Bela Kun addressing the crowds, 1919.

Meanwhile, the Romanian army, having fended off Hungary's invasion of Transylvania, counterattacked. With enemy forces bearing down on Budapest, Kun appealed to Lenin to send reinforcements. But with the Russian Bolsheviks engaged in fighting the counterrevolutionaries, the 'Whites', in the Russian Civil War, no help was forthcoming. On 1 August, Bela Kun and his men fled to Austria bemoaning that the 'Hungarian proletariat betrayed us'.

The Hungarian Soviet Republic was finished; it had lasted just 133 days.

From Austria, Bela Kun ended up back in the Soviet Union. He fought in the Russian Civil War and, with Lenin's approval, was responsible for the execution of some 50,000 'White' prisoners-of-war who had surrendered on the promise of amnesty. During the 1930s, Kun, along with many other communist leaders, fell victim to Stalin's purges and was executed some point during August 1938.

The Horthy Years

On 16 November 1919, three months after the fall of the Soviet Republic, Hungary's National Army marched into Budapest. Following the 'Red Terror', came the period of 'White Terror', when counterrevolutionaries sought revenge and terrorized communists and supporters of Kun's regime – and Jews. Kun was a Jew and likewise many of his closest associates, thus, in the perverse logic of the counterrevolutionaries, all Jews were suspect and hence vulnerable to the White Terror.

The Romanian army remained stationed in Hungary until 25 February 1920 when, following orders from the Allied powers, they evacuated. Meantime, the National Army took control. At its head was Admiral Miklós Horthy, the wartime commander-in-chief of Hungary's Imperial Fleet. Following the Treaty of Trianon, Hungary had become a landlocked nation and Horthy's services as an admiral were no longer needed. Instead, he became head of the National Army.

With a coalition of right-wing parties taking control, Hungary returned to being a constitutional monarchy. The obvious choice for monarch was Hungary's last king, Charles IV. But the Allies vetoed the proposal, not wanting to have a former Habsburg as the Hungarian monarch. Instead, the coalition asked Miklós Horthy to act as regent, 'representing' Charles. (Indeed, Horthy blocked Charles' subsequent attempts to return to Hungary). Horthy accepted and the Kingdom of Hungary was founded on 1 March 1920. Horthy's appointment was to last until the government had appointed a king, one acceptable to the Allies. But it never happened and Horthy retained power as regent and virtual dictator for 24 years.

Thus, peculiarly, for almost a quarter of a century, Hungary was a kingdom without a king.

Miklós Horthy, c1943.

During the 1920s, Horthy, together with his prime minister, István Bethlen, tried to reverse the terms of the Treaty of Trianon and stabilise Hungary's economy. They were unsuccessful in the former and their economic efforts were ultimately in vain following the Great Depression which followed the Wall Street Crash on 24 October 1929.

In 1931, Bethlen resigned to be replaced by the openly-fascist and anti-Semitic Gyula Gömbös who took office on condition, as laid down by Horthy, that he tone down his anti-Semitism. (Bethlen died in a Moscow prison in 1946). But under Gömbös' direction, Hungary moved closer to both Benito Mussolini's fascist Italy and Adolf Hitler's Nazi Germany. A trade agreement with Germany certainly helped Hungary's economic recovery but made Hungary more reliant on Germany.

Gömbös died in 1936. His successors maintained the links he'd made with Italy and Germany, and under Hitler's influence, Hungary became increasingly nationalistic, totalitarian and anti-Semitic, enacting several anti-Semitic laws. 5.1 per cent of Hungary's population were Jewish and almost 25 per cent in the capital. But up to half the white-collared professions, judges, lawyers, doctors, teachers, etc., were Jewish. A 'Second Jewish Law', 1939, followed Hitler's lead and defined Jews by race instead of religion. Further laws limited the number of Jews allowed to attend university, partake in white-collared professions, and forbade intercourse between Jews and non-Jews. Opponents of one of Gömbös' successors, the anti-Semitic Béla Imrédy, prime minister from 1938, discovered that he was of Jewish ancestry, and in February 1939 was forced to resign.

In March 1938, Hitler, through a process called *Anschluss*, unified Austria and Germany into one. Hungary now bordered the German Reich. Horthy drew closer to Hitler, believing the German chancellor was the only man capable of returning to Hungary the lands it lost at Trianon. But Horthy was strong enough to resist Hitler's demand that Hungary participate in his planned takeover of the Sudetenland, until that point part of Czechoslovakia. Nevertheless, following Hitler's successful annexation of the Sudetenland in September 1938, Hitler allowed Hungary to annex south-east Slovakia. Horthy made his triumphal entrance in Slovakia, declaring, 'As I passed along the roads, people embraced one another, fell upon their knees, and wept with joy because liberation had come to them at last, without war, without bloodshed'. But the price was high – Horthy had signed a pact with the devil, aligning Hungary's interests firmly into Germany's orbit.

Miklós Horthy and Adolf Hitler, 1938.

In February 1939, Hungary added its signature to the Anti-Comintern Pact, an anti-communist pact originally agreed in 1936 between Nazi Germany and Japan; and two months later, again following

Germany's lead, withdrew from the League of Nations.

On 1 September 1939, Germany invaded Poland. Two days' later, both Great Britain and France declared war on Germany. The Second World War had started.

Hungary's prime minister, Pal Teleki, refused Germany access to Poland through Hungary. As a result, Poland viewed Hungary as a friendly state, and thousands of Polish soldiers and hundreds of thousands of civilians managed to escape the Nazis by crossing the border into Hungary.

Nevertheless, within four weeks, Poland had surrendered.

Hitler's early advances were spectacularly successful. Within a matter of seven months, Germany had defeated Poland, Norway, Denmark, the Netherlands, Belgium, Luxemburg and France. On 27 September 1940, Germany, Italy and Japan formed a military alliance, the Tripartite Pact. Two months' later, on 20 November, under German pressure, Pal Teleki added his signature (as did Romania, Slovakia and Bulgaria).

Adolf Hitler, Galeazzo Ciano (Benito Mussolini's foreign minister and son-in-law) and Pal Teleki (wearing glasses) at the signing of the Tripartite Pact, 20 November 1940.

In August 1940, thanks to Hitler, Hungary regained northern Transylvania from Romania, an area of consisting of 2.2 million inhabitants, 50 per cent being Magyar.

Hitler intended to invade Yugoslavia and again sought Pál Teleki's permission to march his armies through Hungary. Despite signing the Tripartite Pact just a few months' before, Teleki refused. Just four months' before, he'd signed an 'eternal friendship' treaty with Yugoslavia. But Teleki knew if he didn't yield to Hitler's demands, then Hungary would be next in Germany's firing line. At the same time, adding to the pressure, Britain warned Teleki that it would declare war on Hungary if Teleki gave in to Hitler. It was too much for the beleaguered prime minister. On 3 April, he shot himself.

Pál Teleki's legacy remains controversial in Hungary. Yes, he stood-up to Hitler in 1939 and tried to do so again two years' later. But it was Teleki that had signed-in many of Hungary's anti-Semitic laws.

With Horthy's approval, Teleki's replacement allowed Hitler to launch part of Germany's invasion of Yugoslavia from Hungarian soil. As promised, Hungary regained further territory thus, by mid-1941, Hungary's territory had almost doubled from the amount assigned by the Treaty of Trianon in 1920, regaining 2.3 million Magyars in the process. Horthy was delighted.

On 22 June 1941, Germany invaded the Soviet Union. A week later, Hungary joined the fight on Germany's side.

By now, Horthy was having second thoughts, realising the folly of having joined forces with Hitler.

Together with his third wartime prime minister, Miklós Kállay, Horthy refused Germany's demands to deport its Jews to Germany's death camps. Hungary's Jews may have been subject to anti-Semitic laws and Horthy may have declared himself an anti-Semite but he was not prepared to send them to their deaths. He ordered Kállay to secretly negotiate with the Western Allies. The utter elimination of Hungary's Second Army at the Battle of Stalingrad in January 1943 confirmed for Horthy that he was now on the losing side and that it wouldn't be too long before Stalin's Red Army were at Hungary's borders.

Once Hitler became aware of Horthy's treachery, he acted. On 15 March 1944, Hitler invited Horthy to a meeting in Salzburg. It was merely a trick to get Horthy out of the country while, on 19 March, Hitler's armies invaded Hungary.

Horthy was told his country would be treated as an enemy and subject to complete occupation unless Hungary co-operated with Germany. And the first thing Horthy had to do was to replace Prime Minister Kállay with someone pro-German. The man chosen was Döme Sztójay. (Kállay was deported to

Mauthausen concentration camp in Austria but survived).

Horthy may still have been regent and Sztójay his prime minister but now the Nazis were in charge, and Hungary's economy geared-up to help Germany's war. And in came the notorious Adolf Eichmann.

Adolf Eichmann, 1942.

In just an eight-week period in mid-1944, Eichmann, with Sztójay's help, organised the transportation of 437,402 Jews to the death camps, some 12,000 per day, all but 15,000 to Auschwitz. Indeed, almost half the Jews killed at Auschwitz were Hungarian. (Eichmann, proud of his work, once declared, 'I will leap into my grave laughing with the knowledge that five million enemies of the Reich have died like animals').

In July 1944, Horthy, under pressure from the Western Allies, sacked Sztójay and managed to put a stop to the deportations. On 15 October 1944, Horthy agreed an armistice with the Soviet Union. But Hitler wasn't finished yet. A crack commando team kidnapped Horthy's son, also called Miklós, and smuggled him into Germany. At gunpoint, Horthy was ordered to renounce the armistice with the Soviet Union and abdicate in favour of Arrow Cross leader, Ferenc Szálasi. If he refused, he was told, his son would be killed. He signed. Horthy was then also taken to Germany and kept hostage, albeit in comfortable circumstances.

(Miklós Horthy, Jr. was sent to Dachau concentration camp but survived the war. After the war, his father, Horthy, Snr., was interned at Nuremberg prison until December 1945. He moved to Bavaria and in 1950, along with his son, emigrated to Portugal where he lived in quiet retirement, wrote his memoirs, and died aged 88 in 1957. Horthy Jr. remained in Portugal, dying in 1993).

A Jewish couple with yellow stars, Budapest, 1945. Fortepan.

The ardent anti-Semitic, Nazi-inspired Arrow Cross party had been founded in 1935. For its entire existence, its leader was Ferenc Szálasi who now, in October 1944, found himself Hungary's head of state. In power for just 163 days, from 15 October 1944 to 28 March 1945, Szálasi sanctioned the resumption of Jewish deportations and murder of up to 15,000 Jews. Many were killed in Budapest on the banks of the River Danube where they were ordered to remove their shoes before being shot.

But the Red Army was already within Hungarian borders at the point Szálasi had taken charge. On 26 December, Soviet and Romanian troops surrounded Budapest and subjected it to a siege that cost the lives of some 25,000 civilians and the destruction of over a quarter of the city's buildings. The siege lasted until 13 February 1945 with the surrender of the capital. Fighting continued throughout the country for another seven weeks until 4 April when the Red Army liberated Hungary from Nazi rule. The war in Hungary was officially over.

But a peaceful existence was still a long way off for the people of Hungary, especially its women. According to calculations made by the Red Cross, the Soviet liberators mass raped up to some 200,000

Hungarian women and girls. (This, out of a population of 4.5 million females).

Ferenc Szálasi.

Ferenc Szálasi fled to Austria where he was captured by American troops and returned to Hungary. He was hanged in Budapest on 12 March 1946.

Post-war

Hungary may have been spared the onslaught of war until 1944, but post-war, its economy lay in ruin. Half of Hungary's industrial capacity was devastated and some 90 per cent damaged. Railway lines and trains were destroyed. What little survived had either been taken by the Nazis back to Germany or seized as reparations by the Soviets. The government responded to the financial chaos by simply printing more money. The result was the worst hyperinflation in modern history; dwarfing that experienced in Weimar Germany in the early 1920s: in March 1941, there were five Hungarian pengös to the US dollar; by the summer of 1946 that had risen to 460,000,000,000,000,000,000,000,000 pengös to the US dollar (that's 460 septillion). In other words, money had become meaningless. The pengö was, at that point, replaced by the forint.

Joseph Stalin and the Western Allies had joined forces during the war in order to defeat Hitler. With the war now over, the uneasy and false wartime alliance fell away to reveal the degree of mutual suspicion that had lain dormant while Hitler remained alive. It was each other they now viewed as the main threat to their security. In the closing months of the war and the immediate post-war years, a number of European nations found themselves political pawns in the struggle for hegemony and influence, not least Hungary. At the Yalta Conference in February 1945, Stalin signed a document called the 'Declaration of Liberated Europe', in which nations that had been 'former Axis state(s) in Europe' would be encouraged to hold 'free elections ... responsive to the will of the people'. Stalin knew his communist parties stood no chance of electoral success. Sure enough, in the national Hungarian elections of November 1945, the communists came third, polling a mere 17 per cent, losing heavily to the Smallholders' Party who won 57 per cent.

Joseph Stalin, c1942. Library of Congress.

Hungary's communists were not unduly perturbed by their crushing defeat. Their leader, Matyas Rakosi, the self-styled 'Stalin's best pupil', who had told Stalin to expect a 60 to 70 per cent share of the vote, confidently reckoned that the defeat would 'not play an important role in Communist plans'.

Matyas Rakosi was born one of eleven children to Jewish parents in 1892 in a village called Ada, now in Serbia but then part of the Austro-Hungarian Empire. Rakosi hated all forms of religion, including his own Judaism, and became a fervent anti-Semite. A polyglot, Rakosi could speak eight languages. He served in the Austro-Hungarian army during the First World War, being taken prisoner on the Eastern Front by the Russians, and held for years in a prisoner of war camp during which time he converted to communism. Returning home in 1918 as a member of the Hungarian Communist Party, he was given command of the Red Guard during the 133-day Hungarian Soviet Republic formed by Bela Kun in 1919. Following the collapse of the republic, Rakosi fled to Austria, then onto Moscow.

In 1924, Stalin sent Rakosi back to Hungary with instructions to re-establish the Hungarian Communist Party which had been forced underground by Horthy's new regime. Rakosi was arrested in 1927, and sentenced to eight years' imprisonment, which, later, was extended to life. But in November 1940, after 13 years in a Hungarian prison, he was released – in exchange for a set of symbolic Hungarian flags and banners that had been stored in a Moscow museum since their capture in 1849. Again, Rakosi returned to Moscow to prepare for the next stage in the communist struggle for power in his homeland.

Matyas Rakosi, June 1948. Fortepan.

When, in April 1945, at the end of the Second World War, Stalin's Red Army liberated Hungary from Nazi control, Rakosi again returned to Hungary and served as General Secretary for the Hungarian communists.

Despite the communists' electoral defeat in 1945, the Soviets still had huge influence and their representative in Hungary, Kliment Voroshilov, pressurized the Smallholders' Party into forming a coalition government in which the communists were allocated four out of the 18 cabinet posts. The Smallholders' Party, who, having won 57 per cent, could have ruled alone, found themselves with just half the cabinet.

On 1 February 1946, the Kingdom of Hungary was abolished, officially replaced by the Second Republic of Hungary. The leader of the Smallholders' Party, Zoltán Tildy, became president, and Ferenc Nagy was named prime minister with Rákosi deputy prime minister.

Dedicated communist László Rajk, a veteran of the Spanish Civil War, was appointed minister of the interior and under his aegis established the Hungarian security police (AVH), which soon began arresting leaders of the Smallholders' Party, charging them with 'crimes against the Republic'. Based in the same building used by the Arrow Cross in Budapest's Andrassy Street, Rakosi and Rajk had no qualms about using former Arrow Cross torturers to work for the AVH. These men, the 'little fascists', as Rakosi called them, 'aren't such bad fellows'. (The building now houses the 'House of Terror' museum).

László Rajk in front of a picture of Matyas Rakosi, May 1947. Fortepan.

In May 1947, on Rajk's orders, the ÁVH kidnapped Ferenc Nagy's son. Nagy resigned as prime minister, got his son back, and, having been given a huge sum of money, emigrated to the US. His successor, Lajos Dinnyés, knowing his place, was little more than a puppet in Rakosi's hands.

The communists prepared for the next set of elections – August 1947. Despite rigging the election and committing blatant electoral fraud, and despite winning with 22.25 per cent, they still failed to gain an overall majority. (The Smallholders' Party's share of the vote fell to 15 per cent).

With Voroshilov never far behind him, Rakosi forced the Social Democrats to merge with the communists, becoming the Hungarian Working People's Party, declaring all other parties illegal and arresting every potential opponent of the party. Thereby Rakosi gained power, later boasting that he had cut up his opponents one-by-one like 'slices of salami'. On 20 August 1949, the Second Republic of Hungary had officially become the People's Republic of Hungary with Rákosi at its helm.

Pro-government parade in Budapest, 1950, bearing portraits of Vladimir Lenin, Matyas Rakosi and Joseph Stalin. Fortepan.

With the communists in power, Soviet ideology now pervaded every sphere of Hungarian society – workers and peasants had to attend political lectures, religious schools were nationalized and every schoolchild obliged to learn Russian. The party was severely purged, with almost a half of its middling ranks dismissed or arrested. Under Matyas Rakosi's rule of terror, some 2,000 Hungarians were executed and up to 100,000 imprisoned or deported east. And this in a country with less than 10 million inhabitants.

Those considered bourgeois were forced out of their homes and moved into dilapidated rural dwellings. Anti-capitalist laws deprived 'capitalists' their businesses. Farmers were forced against their will to join collectives. Those who resisted were beaten or imprisoned. The AVH arrested some 225 Catholic priests and, most notoriously, arrested the popular Cardinal Joseph Mindszenty.

Cardinal Mindszenty was born Joseph Pehm in 1892 in the Hungarian village of Csehi-Mindszent (the name which, in 1941, Pehm adopted), and was ordained a priest in 1915 at the age of 23. He spoke out against Hungary's short-lived Soviet Republic and was subsequently arrested and imprisoned until its collapse in August 1919.

In March 1944, during the Second World War, he was consecrated as a bishop but later the same year was again imprisoned, this time by the Arrow Cross government for protesting against Hungary's treatment and oppression of its Jewish population.

Following the war, Mindszenty was appointed Primate of Hungary and Archbishop of Esztergom, and in 1946 was made a cardinal by Pope Pius XII.

But by now the Hungarian communist party was looking to take power.

Mindszenty opposed Rakosi's regime and was known for his vocal criticism. The cardinal toured the country, urging people to resist the government's plan to nationalise the church's land and property and Hungary's 4,813 Catholic schools. In a letter published in November 1948 and broadcast on the Voice of America radio station, the cardinal said, 'I stand for God, for the Church and for Hungary. Compared with the sufferings of my people, my own fate is of no importance. I do not accuse my accusers … I pray for those who, in the words of Our Lord, "know not what they do". I forgive them from the bottom of my heart.'

On 26 December 1948, Mindszenty was arrested. Alternatively, stripped naked or dressed as a clown, Mindszenty was tortured, methods that included sleep deprivation, beatings, intense and incessant noise, and forced fed mind-altering drugs. Finally, after continuous torture, the cardinal signed his confession.

Cardinal Mindszenty taking an open-air confession, Budapest, 1938. Fortepan.

Mindszenty appeared at his show trial washed, shaved and dressed up in a new suit. He was accused of over forty farcical wrongdoings, such as planning to steal the Hungarian crown jewels and, according to the prosecution, of inciting the 'American imperialists to declare war on our country'. 'I am guilty on principle and in detail of most of the accusations made,' he said, but denied that he was trying to topple the government. The verdict, of course, was a foregone conclusion, and after the six-day trial, on 8 February 1949, Cardinal Mindszenty was found guilty of treason.

Escaping the death sentence (the communists wanted to avoid having a dead martyr on their hands), he was sentenced to life imprisonment.

The verdict outraged the free world. Pope Pius XII, who excommunicated all those involved in the trial, called the outcome a 'serious outrage which inflicts a deep wound . . . on every upholder of the dignity and liberty of man'. US president, Harry S Truman, said it was 'one of the black spots on Hungary's history and a blot upon the nation'.

Meanwhile, while Rakosi may have been effective in the murderous business of politics, he had no talent for running the country. His policies of collectivization, modelled on that of the Soviet Union's, failed miserably, causing economic ruin. In 1950, he launched his Five-Year-Plan, a favourite ploy of communist governments everywhere. His aim was to increase Hungary's productivity by 380 per cent. It also failed spectacularly – output fell, wages fell and, most devastatingly, food supply plummeted causing widespread famine. The fact that Hungary had agreed to pay the Soviet Union war reparations to the tune of 20 per cent of Hungary's annual income did not help. Civilians were all obliged to buy state bonds, further diminishing their income. But while Stalin remained alive, Rakosi's position was secure.

But on 5 March 1953, Stalin died. Across Eastern Europe, people officially mourned. Shops closed, churches rang their bells, newspapers appeared adorned with a black border, radio stations played nothing but solemn music.

In July, within four months of Stalin's death, Rakosi was sacked. Lavrenty Beria, Stalin's former head of his secret police, accused Rakosi of conducting a 'wave of oppression' against his own people, which was rather rich, given Beria's murderous reputation. Rakosi was replaced by the reformist and populist, Imre Nagy.

A bald-headed man with a walrus moustache, 'Uncle Imre' as Nagy was sometimes known, was born 7 June 1896 in the town of Kaposvár in southern Hungary. He worked as a locksmith before joining the Austro-Hungarian army during the First World War. In 1915, he was captured and spent much of the war as a prisoner in Russia. He escaped and, having converted to communism, joined the Red Army and fought alongside the Bolsheviks during the Russian Revolution of 1917.

Imre Nagy, 1945. Fortepan.

In 1918, Nagy returned to Hungary as a committed communist and served Bela Kun's short-lived Soviet Republic. Following its collapse in August 1919, after only five months, Nagy, as with other former members of Kun's regime, lived underground, liable to arrest. Eventually, in 1928, he fled to Austria and from there, in 1930, to the Soviet Union, where he spent the next fourteen years studying agriculture.

Following the Second World War, Nagy returned again to Hungary serving as Minister of Agriculture in Hungary's post-war communist government. Loyal to Stalin, Nagy led the charge of collectivization, redistributing the landowners' land to the peasants.

A *New York Times* journalist, writing in 1956, described Nagy as a 'burly 6-foot 200-pounder… He never made any secret of his fondness for good food, good drink, good clothes. He liked to sit in Budapest cafes and discuss politics or the merits of different Hungarian football teams'.

Following his appointment as chairman in July 1953, Nagy tried to usher in a move away from Moscow's influence and introduce a period of liberalism and political and economic reform. He sanctioned the release of political prisoners, and proposed to bring to an end Hungary's rapid industrialization and an end to collectivization. Thus, Nagy became something of a one-off – a communist politician who was actually admired and liked by the people.

But, of course, it made him equally hated by his colleagues, especially Rakosi. And as far as the Kremlin was concerned, Nagy was going too far with his reforms and setting a bad example to other countries within the Eastern Bloc. Nagy quickly became too popular for the Kremlin's liking and in April 1955 Rákosi was put back in charge and the terror and oppression started anew. Seven months later, Nagy was expelled from the communist party altogether.

In June 1956, Rakosi was replaced again – this time by fellow hardline Stalinist, Erno Gero.

The Kremlin, finally realising how unpopular Rakosi was, told him to resign on grounds of ill health and fly to Moscow for treatment. He did, never to return to his home country. He was not missed. Streets and buildings bearing Rakosi's name were promptly re-named. In 1962, Rakosi suffered the ultimate indignity when he was expelled from the

Hungarian Communist Party, the organisation he'd spent his life working for. He died in Gorky (modern-day Nizhny Novgorod), aged 78, in February 1971.

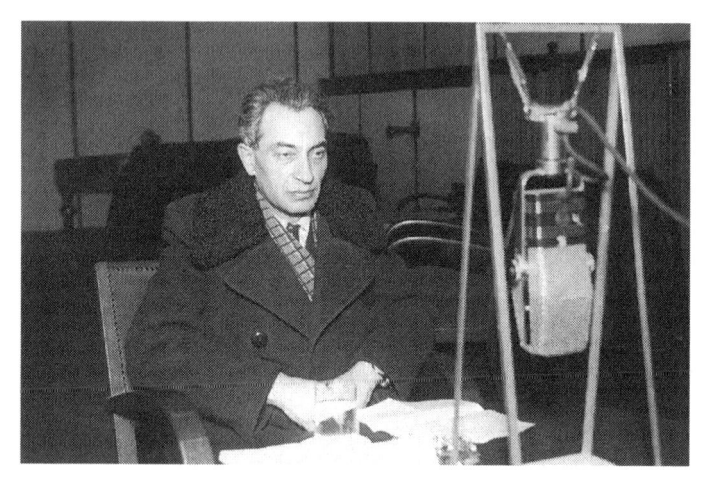

Erno Gero in the studio of the Hungarian Radio, 1955. Fortepan.

Meanwhile, following Rakosi's dismissal and Gero's appointment, Cardinal Mindszenty was transferred from prison to house arrest.

Post-Stalin

A new post-Stalinist era beckoned for those trapped behind the Iron Curtain. But if the workers of East Germany thought that Stalin's death meant change, they were soon disabused as the East German premier, Walter Ulbricht, strove to increase industrial output.

Walter Ulbricht, like Rakosi, was a Stalinist to the core. East Germany's head of state from 1950 to 1973, he was an unusually dull man, devoid of personality, devoted to the socialist cause, but with no empathy for the working masses, the very people he was supposedly fighting for. Speaking in Berlin in

June 1961, he infamously said: 'No one has any intention of building a wall'. Two months' later, the Berlin Wall went up. Even Lavrenty Beria described Ulbricht as the 'greatest idiot' that he had ever met. And Alexander Dubcek, Czechoslovakian leader during the 1968 Prague Spring, called Ulbricht, 'a dogmatist fossilized somewhere in Stalin's period', adding, 'I found him personally repugnant'. Another contemporary described Ulbricht as a 'nasty, drab, tale-teller of a bureaucrat'.

In 1953, with East Germany's economy stagnating and hundreds of East Berliners migrating to West Berlin on a daily basis, Ulbricht proposed a range of measures to pump-up the economy – increase taxes, increase prices and increase production by 10 per cent – but with no corresponding increase in wages. If the new quotas were not met, workers were told, wages would be cut by a third. The Kremlin viewed these proposals with concern, advising Ulbricht to tone down the measures and slow down the intense pace of industrialisation that the East German leader insisted was necessary. For the workers of the German Democratic Republic this was a lose-lose scenario.

Citizens of post-war Eastern Europe did as their governments ordered, any protest was silent, whispered in dark corners. But these measures were too much; Ulbricht had gone too far.

Walter Ulbricht, c1946. Deutsche Fotothek.

On 16 June 1953, East Berlin construction workers downed tools. The following morning, 17 June, the strike had spread with over 40,000 demonstrators marching through the capital. Their demands at first focussed on the economic – a return to the old work quotas. But then as the strike spread to other cities – Leipzig, Dresden and some 400 cities and towns throughout East Germany, their voices gained strength and their hearts courage. They demanded increasingly more – free elections, a new government, democracy. Meetings were held; workers' councils elected, Russian bookshops burnt down. In the East German town of Merseburg, workers stormed the police station and released prisoners from the jails.

Protestors tore down communist flags and carried banners proclaiming, 'We want free elections; we are not slaves', 'Death to communism' and 'Long Live Eisenhower'. This was no longer a strike but an uprising.

Ulbricht turned to the Kremlin. Lavrenty Beria, the man poised to take over now that Stalin was dead, sent in the tanks. The crews, 20,000 troops based in East Germany, were told by Beria not to 'spare bullets'. This was a revolution and it needed crushing.

Martial law was declared while, on the afternoon of the 17th, the tanks moved in and, alongside the East German police, opened fire. Down the Unter den Linden, people, demonstrators, civilians fell. How many were killed no one knows for sure. The figures vary considerably between sources based in the West and those of the East. But at least 40 were killed, possibly up to 260, and 400 wounded.

Protestors on the streets of Leipzig during the East German Uprising, 17 June 1953. German Federal Archives.

If the East German protestors hoped for assistance from the West, they were to be disappointed. The US was not prepared to risk war over such an issue. But it did start a food aid programme, distributing over 5 million food parcels during July and August. Winston Churchill's response, at the time prime minister, was also muted. Churchill may have feared the resurgence of a united Germany so soon after the Second World War: while publicly supporting a united Germany, a divided one, he felt, was more secure. Churchill considered the regime's response to the uprising as 'restrained'.

Thus without the West's intervention, pockets of resistance continued for a few weeks but the main thrust of the East German Uprising had been crushed within just 24 hours of starting.

And then came the reprisals – thousands arrested, perhaps up to 6,000, tortured and interned. Six ringleaders were executed. Walter Ulbricht took the opportunity of purging his party of seventy per cent of its members.

Following Stalin's death, the fearsome Lavrenty Beria looked set to replace him. But his politburo colleagues in the Kremlin had other ideas. On 26 June 1953, Beria was arrested on trumped-up charges, such as spying for the British, put on trial, found guilty and executed on 23 December 1953.

Instead, Nikita Khrushchev took Stalin's place as general secretary.

On 25 February 1956, Khrushchev delivered a speech to a closed session of party leaders in which he dismantled the legend of the recently-deceased Joseph Stalin and criticized almost every aspect of Stalin's method of rule. The speech entitled 'On the Cult of the Individual and Its Consequences' would become known as simply Khrushchev's 'Secret Speech'.

Nikita Khrushchev, centre, shaking hands with Walter Ulbricht, 11 July 1958. German Federal Archives.

For over four hours, Khrushchev denounced Stalin's methods, his abuse of power and criticized the regime built on 'suspicion, fear and terror'.

Khrushchev, aware of the impact his words were having, described how Stalin had chosen 'the path of repression and physical annihilation'. He described Stalin as a 'very distrustful man, sickly suspicious ... He could look at a man and say: "Why are your eyes so shifty today?"'

Khrushchev damned Stalin's 'cruel repressions' and highlighted the catalogue of Stalin's terror, starting with the assassination in December 1934 of Sergei Kirov, Stalin's man in Leningrad, implying that Kirov had not been the victim of a counterrevolutionary conspiracy, as always maintained, but that Stalin, fearful of Kirov's increasing popularity, had sanctioned Kirov's murder himself.

He condemned Stalin's conduct during the war, calling Stalin a coward who 'not once… visited the front during the whole war'. Stalin refused to take seriously warnings, even from Winston Churchill, that Hitler was planning an invasion of the Soviet Union. Indeed, the shock was such that days after the Nazi invasion, Stalin suffered something akin to a breakdown.

Khrushchev described the 'deathly hush' that followed his speech as his pale-faced audience absorbed the heretical attack on the man who had ruled over them for so long. Many cried. 'De-Stalinization' had started.

The text of Khrushchev's secret speech, although not officially made public in the Soviet Union until 1988, soon spread across Russia and abroad, causing shock that the great man's name should be so besmirched but also relief that, through Khrushchev's speech, the tyranny that had overshadowed the Soviet Union for so long was now something of the past. On hearing the speech, the former Polish president, Bolesław Bierut, was so shocked he died of a heart attack.

But the speech caused riots in Georgia, Stalin's country of birth, where they still viewed him as a hero: 'Glory to the great Stalin,' they chanted.

Following Khrushchev's Secret Speech, the expectation of greater freedom from centralised, Kremlin rule intensified. In June 1956 in Poland, in a repeat of the East German Uprising of 1953, workers revolted demanding economic reform. The Polish government, in a conciliatory gesture to their people, replaced their hard-line leader with the popular and reformist Wladyslaw Gomulka. The Poles had taken Khrushchev at his word and were following a 'different road to socialism'.

Protestors in Poznan, Poland, bearing a banner 'We demand bread', June 1956.

Khrushchev was not impressed. Furious, he flew unannounced to Warsaw for a showdown with the Poles. Gomulka held his ground but promised that

Poland would remain loyal to Moscow and remain a committed member of the Warsaw Pact. Satisfied with this, Khrushchev withdrew. Meanwhile, in Hungary, people were asking – if the Poles could do it, why couldn't they?

Speaking in 1957, Peter Fryer, member of Great Britain's communist party, described the situation in pre-revolutionary Hungary: 'Hypocrisy without limit; medieval cruelty; dogmas and slogans devoid of life or meaning; national pride outraged; poverty for all but a tiny handful of leaders who lived in luxury, with mansions on *Rózsadomb*, Budapest's pleasant Hill of Roses, special schools for their children, special well-stocked shops for their wives – even special bathing beaches at Lake Balaton, shut off from the common people by barbed wire.' (Peter Fryer resigned from the communist party over what happened in Hungary in 1956.)

The spark that lit the torch paper of revolution in Hungary was the re-burial of a man who had been instrumental in the oppression of Hungarians. Communist regimes are notoriously adept at destroying their most ardent puppets, and Hungary's

László Rajk is one such example. As head of the feared AVH, he oversaw a number of show trials, and, working under Rakosi, had thousands arrested. But Rakosi feared Rajk and in 1949 had his AVH chief arrested and severely tortured. Subjected to his own show trial, Rajk 'confessed' to various ludicrous charges, such as plotting to overthrow the 'democratically' elected government, of being an agent of Western imperialists, and behind a plot to kill Rakosi. The outcome was never in doubt – Rajk was found guilty and, aged 40, executed on 15 October 1949, his body dumped in an unmarked grave. Rajk's widow, Julia, was sentenced to five years' imprisonment.

But then, in 1956, as Rakosi's star began to fade, László Rajk was rehabilitated. On 27 June 1956, Julia Rajk, recently released from prison, spoke to a meeting of Hungarian writers and intellectuals in Budapest. She told her audience that Horthy's jails were much better than Rakosi's. 'They killed my husband, and tore my little baby from me … These criminals have trampled all sentiment and honesty underfoot.'

On 6 October 1956, three months after Rakosi's forced resignation, Rajk and three executed colleagues were re-buried and laid to rest in Budapest's Kerepesi Cemetery. It was a lavish, five-hour ceremony – black flags hung from buildings, shops and businesses closed for the day and 100,000 people lined the streets and attended the funeral. Guests of honour were Julia Rajk and her seven-year-old son who had been a baby at the time of his father's execution. Noted by his absence was Rakosi's replacement, Erno Gero. One orator savaged the 'sadistic criminals' that had murdered Rajk, men who had 'crawled into the sun from the stinking swamp of a cult of personality'. No one mentioned that Rajk himself, as head of the AVH, had been responsible for the rounding-up, arrest, torture, imprisonment and execution of thousands of Hungarian civilians.

Uprising

For many, László Rajk's funeral on 6 October 1956 marked the end of Stalinism in Hungary. Workers and students across the nation met and discussed the political situation. Students formed democratic unions which would never have been tolerated during Rakosi's time. But, on the whole, good intentions and fine words were not matched by action. A meeting on 22 October attended by 5,000 students in Budapest's Technical College, however, was different. Here, they drew-up a sixteen-point manifesto.

Their demands were, within themselves,

revolutionary and daring in the extreme. They demanded, amongst other things, immediate removal of all Soviet troops from Hungarian soil; election by secret ballot of all Party members; a new government under the direction of Imre Nagy and dismissal of 'all criminal leaders of the Stalin-Rákosi era'; the return of Mátyás Rákosi to face trial before a people's tribunal; national-wide, multi-party elections by universal, secret ballot; non-interference in the internal affairs of one state by another; a minimum living wage for workers; the release and rehabilitation of political prisoners; freedom of opinion and of expression, freedom of the press and of radio; the removal of Stalin's statue in Budapest; the removal of Soviet emblems (to be replaced by the traditional Hungarian arms of Kossuth); and new uniforms for the army which conformed to national traditions.

Satisfied with their evening's work, they agreed to march the following day in support of the Poles, culminating in the laying of wreaths at the statue of Jozef Bem, a Polish general who was one of the leaders of the 1848 Hungarian Revolution and fondly remembered in Hungary.

Ahead of the march, the students began the day of Tuesday 23 October by posting-up stencilled copies of their 16-point manifesto on every available lamppost, tree or shop front. The newspapers had refused to publish them but the students had had access to a sympathetic printing shop. In the afternoon, thousands of students, having gathered at the university, began their march towards General Bem's statue, carrying banners and placards bearing anti-government and anti-Soviet slogans and chanting Imre Nagy's name. Others charged around in vans, using loudspeakers to spread the message. Thousands joined them – shop assistants, office workers, factory workers and even soldiers; people from nearby towns and cities rushed to the capital to join the march. Members of a large literary group, the Petofi Circle, formed a second demonstration and congregated at the statue of their inspiration, the poet Sandor Petofi, who had died fighting for Hungarian independence in 1848, where they recited his most famous poem, *Rise, Magyar*. The demonstrators headed for Parliament Square and, along the way, tore down Soviet flags and Red Stars from public buildings. Shouting 'Russians go home!', they flew the Hungarian flag with its central Soviet emblem torn out.

Demonstrators in Budapest, 23 October 1956. Fortepan.

Panicked, the Minister of the Interior tried to ban the demonstrations but, realising he was impotent against such vast numbers, quickly rescinded the order.

Gathering in Parliament Square, the demonstrators, now numbering some 200,000, called for Nagy, who duly appeared on a balcony. His first word, 'comrades', was greeted by hoots of derision – 'We are no longer "comrades",' came the response, loud and clear. Nagy's speech proved a disappointment – he called for calm and told the demonstrators to go home – not what they wanted to hear.

At 8 p.m., broadcasting on the radio, Gero condemned the 'bourgeois reactionaries' who dared to criticize the glorious communist party and its workings: 'We shall defend the achievements of the people's democracy under all circumstances from whichever quarter they may be threatened. Today the chief aim of the enemies of our people is to shake the power of the working class, to loosen the peasant-worker alliance, to undermine the leadership of the working class in our country and to upset their faith in its party, in the Hungarian Workers' Party.' His words were akin to pouring petrol on a fire. Meanwhile, demonstrators in Heroes' Square attacked the massive statue of Stalin, the statue the students had mentioned in their manifesto.

The 'Stalin Monument', to give it its official name, had been erected as a 'monumental gift' to the Hungarian people on the occasion of Stalin's seventieth birthday, 21 December 1949. It was built on the site of a church that had been demolished specifically to accommodate the statue. It was certainly an imposing sight: made of bronze, the statue stood 26 foot tall on a 13 foot-high limestone pedestal on top of a 20-foot high tribune. So, altogether the work measured 59 feet (18 metres) in height – the equivalent roughly of a six-storey building. The tribune featured depictions of happy Hungarian citizens, soldiers, workers and mothers bearing children, extending the hand of friendship towards the Soviet leader.

The Stalin Monument, Budapest, 1953. Fortepan.

A newspaper report declared that Stalin: 'will be with us even more. He will watch over our work, and his smile will show us the way. I have been told that in Moscow it is customary to pay a visit to Comrade Lenin (the Lenin Mausoleum) in Red Square before beginning, or after finishing, an important task, either to report or to ask his advice. Undoubtedly the same will occur here with the statue of Comrade Stalin'.

The sculptor was Sándor Mikus, who had entered a competition and, as a result, had won the commission, which made him, according to the Hungarian press, the 'happiest Hungarian sculptor'. It must have been a difficult time for Mikus. He had to get it right. The price of failure would have been high – very high. Mikus knew this and as a result suffered from repeated nightmares in which Stalin appeared to him.

People, on the whole, rather liked the statue as a work of art but despised what it symbolised. Not only did it represent the nation's suppression, it was rumoured that the bronze had been melted down from several former statues of men still highly-regarded by the people but reviled by the regime.

Mikus portrayed Stalin as a man of destiny, with his right arm outstretched, and was praised for having depicted Stalin as 'great in his simplicity and simple in his greatness'.

The decapitated head of Stalin's monument, Budapest, 23 October 1956. Fortepan.

The head of Budapest's police, Sandor Kopacsi, described how demonstrators managed to bring the statue toppling to the ground: 'The demonstrators placed a thick steel rope around the neck of the 25-metre tall Stalin's statue while other people, arriving in trucks with oxygen cylinders and metal cutting blowpipes, were setting to work on the statue's bronze shoes ... An hour later, at precisely 9.37 p.m., the statue fell down from its pedestal'. All that remained of the statue were Stalin's boots on the plinth. People hammered at the statue, decapitating its head, and hacked at the bronze for souvenirs. (Sandor Kopacsi was one of many senior figures who defected to the side of the insurgents. The most senior army officer to defect was Colonel Pal Maleter, a tall, imposing figure, who, based in the Kilian Barracks in central Budapest, co-ordinated teams of insurgents).

Meanwhile, still on the evening of the 23rd, a delegation of protestors tried to broadcast their demands on national radio, arguing that the radio should belong to the people. Rumours spread that those inside the Radio Building had been pinned down by the AVH, and demonstrators gathered to demand their release. The AVH officers responded by throwing tear gas from the windows but it wasn't enough to dislodge the protestors. Instead, they opened fire and killed several civilians. One demonstrator, having been shot dead, was wrapped in the Hungarian flag and held aloft above the crowd.

Fighting continued throughout the night. By the following morning, the insurgents had control of the radio building but at the cost of 16 lives.

At 2 a.m., at Gero's request and on Khrushchev's authorization, two divisions of Soviet tank units stationed nearby began arriving in the capital. Directing manoeuvres from Moscow was Georgi Zhukov, the Soviet hero of the Great Patriotic War (as the Second World War is known in Russia) and now Khrushchev's defence minister. Martial law was imposed. What had begun as a peaceful demonstration had turned very quickly into a full-scale revolution. Fighting took place throughout Budapest and soon spread to other cities in Hungary.

In the early hours of Wednesday 24 October, the Kremlin put Imre Nagy back in charge, believing that 'limited concessions' were necessary to satisfy the Hungarian people. Nagy promised his people reform in return for an end to the violence.

The tanks, when they came, mainly the Russian T-54, lacked mobility and without infantry support were liable to attack. Many Hungarian soldiers, ripping the Soviet insignia from their uniforms, sided with the protestors and armed the insurgents with guns and rifles, while the makeshift Molotov cocktails proved highly effective against the lumbering Soviet tanks trapped in Budapest's narrow side streets. Insurgents smeared the roads with oil and grease in order to make the tanks skid. They hung saucepans from telegraph wires which, from the inside of a tank, looked like anti-tank devices. The T-54s had the word 'petrol' helpfully written on the petrol caps – perfect for twisting open and dropping-in a Molotov cocktail.

Soviet tanks lumbering up a Budapest street, October 1956. Fortepan.

The citizens of Budapest, having taken control of the radio, renamed it Radio Free Kossuth. The state broadcasters were happy to cede control and even confessed to having been instruments of the state: 'We lied by night, we lied by day, we lied on all wavelengths. We, who are before the microphones, are now new men'.

On the morning of the Thursday 25th, thousands gathered in front of the Parliament Building in Budapest's Kossuth Square. Things started off peacefully; indeed there was almost a carnival atmosphere. The demonstrators, having been obliged to learn Russian from an early age, were able to converse and joke with the Soviet tank crews, swapping cigarettes and small gifts. Hungarians climbed aboard the tanks and decked them with the national flag. But then, in an instant, everything changed. Gunshots were heard. AVH men were firing from the rooftops. People stampeded, others were crushed or exposed to gunfire. By the time it was over, there were so many dead, perhaps up to a thousand, their bodies had to be piled-high in undignified heaps in the corners of the square.

Knowing his personal safety could no longer be guaranteed, Gero fled to Moscow. Nagy again appealed for calm and acknowledged the people's despair and anger, expressed sorrow for the Kossuth Square massacre, and vaguely promised reform.

'Russians go home' graffiti on the window of a Russian bookshop, Budapest, October 1956. Fortepan.

But it wasn't enough. Insurgents rampaged through the city, searching for AVH officers. When found, the secret policemen and women suffered a tortuous death, lynched upside down and burnt, their bodies spat upon; punishment for their years of torture and oppression of the Hungarian people. Many of the AVH dead had Stalin and Rakosi postcards pinned to their corpses. A reporter from the *New York Times* recorded the following scene: 'Among those watching this demonstration was a furtive figure clad in a leather coat. Suddenly someone identified him rightly or wrongly as a member of the hated AVH, the Hungarian political police. Like tigers, the crowd turned on him, began to beat him and hustled him into a courtyard. A few minutes later they emerged rubbing their hands with satisfaction. The leather-coated figure was seen no more.'

Insurgents opened the gates of the city's prisons and released and armed the prisoners. They broke into Rakosi's former home and were appalled to find such luxury and opulence. Barricades consisting of ripped-up paving stones, burnt-out vehicles and whatever was at hand were quickly erected on all the main entry points into the city to prevent Soviet reinforcements from entering. The weapons from a deserted munitions factory were seized; petrol was taken from abandoned petrol stations for the Molotov cocktails. Russian street signs were torn down, shops daubed with 'Russians out' slogans, portraits of Stalin and Rakosi torn down and stamped upon. People broke into the AVH offices and burnt files and piles of paper.

Armed insurgents preparing to fight, Budapest, October 1956. Fortepan.

In one of the most notorious massacres outside the capital, over 50 insurgents were gunned down by the AVH on Friday 26 October in the small town of Mosonmagyaróvár, near the Austrian border. Some of the soldiers, unwilling to kill unarmed civilians, aimed low, shooting people in the legs. The following day, a group of Western journalists crossed the border from Austria and were taken to Mosonmagyaróvár where they saw for themselves the scores of wounded men, women and children, and the fifty or so bodies laid out in the town's mortuary. Photographs of the scene were published in newspapers throughout the West. The day after that, armed insurgents from the nearby town of Gyor arrived to seek out those responsible. The attack on the AVH headquarters in Mosonmagyaróvár was equally as brutal and savage.

Meanwhile, in Budapest, fighting continued. The city lay in ruins – buildings badly damaged by Soviet tanks, tramlines buckled, telegraph wires sagging, trees uprooted, pavement stones ripped-up, burnt-out cars and lorries – and Soviet tanks, many of the latter having had the Kossuth coat of arms painted onto them. People everywhere looked like militia – even young children were wearing bullet belts and carrying rifles around. Everywhere, the Hungarian tricolour with the hole in the middle. Bodies of AVH men and women hung from trees; dead civilians and Russian soldiers lay on the ground, their corpses covered with coats and blankets and sprinkled with lime to hide the smell.

A Soviet armoured car in flames, Budapest, October 1956. Fortepan.

But people still had to eat. Queues formed. Sympathetic farmers sent truckloads of food into the cities as gifts for their brave comrades.

The international football match between Hungary and Sweden, due to be played on Sunday 28th, had to be cancelled.

Soviet soldiers dared not leave their tanks. Supplies fell low and their morale plummeted. Holed-up for days on end, the claustrophobic interiors soon stunk of petrol, sweat and excrement. Some T-54s dragged dead Hungarians behind them as a warning to the insurgents.

Imre Nagy was the pivotal figure at this point – being the only state representative the people were prepared to listen to. On Sunday 28 October, Nagy, riding the wave of optimism, called for a ceasefire, promising amnesty for those who took part in the uprising, and promised to negotiate with the uprising's leaders. Again, he acknowledged the people's anger and, most importantly, acknowledged that the unrest was not a counter-revolutionary act, as the Soviets called it, but a legitimate, democratic uprising. He then pledged lots of things – wage increases, the disbanding of the AVH to be replaced by a 'democratic' police force; the immediate removal of Soviet troops from Hungary and even dropping the compulsory greeting of 'comrade'. Fighting stopped and the ceasefire held while people waited for the tanks to withdraw. Hungarians sensed victory. Political parties, long since banned, reformed; new newspapers sprung up, most only a side long, plastered up on shop fronts, trees and street lamps. Soviet war memorials were vandalised, and Russian bookshops destroyed. The scenes in Budapest were repeated elsewhere across the country, not just in the cities but in every town and village – Soviet stars, statues and monuments pulled down, representatives of the government confronted and challenged, demonstrators chanting their demands for democracy and freedom.

Soviet representatives in Budapest endorsed Nagy's proposals. On 29 October, Pal Maleter, the army colonel who had defected to the insurgents' cause, was promoted to general and, more importantly, appointed Defence Minister. This was a significant development – it meant that the rebels had a place and a voice within the cabinet.

Nagy returned to the microphone and promised even more – an immediate coalition government to include representatives from parties long since banned, and even Hungary's withdrawal from the Warsaw Pact, and called on the United Nations to guarantee Hungary's neutrality. This latter point, the intended neutrality, implied that Nagy was not planning on suddenly swapping sides and joining the Western powers. Indeed, he had no intention of being disloyal to Moscow but he did desire greater autonomy for Hungary.

Pal Maleter, c1956. Dutch Federal Archives.

That same day, Cardinal Mindszenty was released: 'the measures depriving Cardinal Primate Joseph Mindszenty of his rights are invalid. The

Cardinal is free to exercise without restriction all his civil and ecclesiastical rights'.

On Tuesday 30 October, Khrushchev withdrew his troops from Hungary – but, unknown to the insurgents, only as far as the border. The people of Budapest began clearing away the worst of the debris, and taking the lime-covered corpses to the cemeteries.

Meanwhile, on 31 October, Khrushchev announced the Soviet government's intention to hold discussions with the Hungarian government on the subject of Soviet troops on Hungarian territory. He even invited Nagy to send over a delegation to Moscow to start the negotiations. The people of Hungary rejoiced – they had done it; they had cowed the Soviet monster; they had forced the Soviet tanks back out of the country.

The following day, 1 November, without informing the Hungarians, Khrushchev changed his mind. Nagy, he concluded, had gone too far; this went much further than Poland. China's Chairman Mao, who had been heckling Khrushchev for being weak, encouraged him to take a firmer line. As Mao pointed out, if Nagy delivered on these reforms, what sort of message would it send to other members of the Eastern Bloc? Its very foundation would be at risk. The Soviet leader decided to fight back after all.

People trying to resume normal lives amongst the ruins of Budapest, November 1956. Fortepan.

On 1 November, receiving reports that Soviet tanks were back on Hungarian soil, Nagy confronted the Soviet Union's ambassador in Hungary, Yuri Andropov. Andropov, who would become USSR's premier from 12 November 1982 to his death, aged 69, on 9 February 1984, assured Nagy that the reports were false – there were no Soviet tanks on Hungarian soil. Indeed, two days' later, the Soviet military command invited a Hungarian government delegation to attend a meeting to discuss the Soviet Union's complete withdrawal from Hungary. The delegation, headed by Pal Maleter, arrived for the meeting. The meeting was nothing more than a ruse – Maleter and his delegation were immediately placed under arrest.

Friday 2 November was All Souls' Day, the day people remember the dead. Church bells rang sombre tones, people lit candles and black flags hung everywhere.

At 9.30 p.m. on 3 November, in an operation codenamed 'Whirlwind', Soviet troops re-entered Hungary and approached the capital. In the early hours of Sunday 4th, the Soviets seized all the vital points of communication. By the time the insurgents had mustered, it was already too late. Together with the Hungarian army, they fought back but this time the Soviets were prepared – infantry, artillery, tanks and even air strikes decimated the city. The tanks reduced to rubble every building from which a single shot was fired.

As the city fell about him, Nagy appeared on Radio Budapest at 5.20 on the morning of 4

November:

'This is Imre Nagy speaking. Today at daybreak Soviet forces started an attack against our capital, obviously with the intention to overthrow the legal Hungarian democratic government. Our troops are still fighting; the Government is still in its place. I notify the people of our country and the entire world of this fact.'

And that was it. Nagy's voice disappeared – no one ever heard it again. Seconds later, the National Anthem played, not the communist version but the anthem that brought tears to patriotic hearts. A couple hours later, at 8.10, Radio Budapest broadcast its last appeal, 'Help Hungary... help, help, help,' before being taken off air.

The 'entire world' that Nagy had appealed to, ignored him. Western powers spoke loud words; the US condemned the attack as a 'monstrous crime'; John Foster Dulles, the US Secretary of State, said, 'To all those suffering under communist slavery, let us say you can count on us'. In the event, the US did nothing – the risks of venturing into an Eastern

European conflict, and the potential for escalation, were too great. Great Britain and France were distracted by the emerging crisis over the Suez Canal and the US by presidential elections. The aid never materialised.

Janos Kadar, c1962. Dutch Federal Archives.

Imre Nagy was replaced by Janos Kadar, a former Interior Minister, who, loyal to Moscow, welcomed the return of Soviet forces to crush the 'counter-revolutionary threat': 'We must put an end to the excesses of the counter-revolutionary elements. The hour for action has sounded. We are going to defend the interest of the workers and peasants and the achievements of the people's democracy'. The insurgents had no longer taken part in a 'legitimate, democratic uprising' but had become 'counter-revolutionaries' again.

Kadar's Soviet-talk was certainly inflammatory. A former communist, now resistance fighter, George Paloczi-Horvath, wrote: 'After our brief span of liberty and democracy, Kadar's hideous slogans and stupid lies, couched in the hated Stalinite terminology, made everyone's blood boil. Although ten million witnesses knew the contrary, the puppet government brought forward the ludicrous lie that our war of liberty was a counter-revolutionary uprising inspired by a handful of fascists'. (Paloczi-Horvath, who had survived five years of torture and solitary confinement in one of Rakosi's jails, managed to escape Hungary at this point and settled in London where he wrote of his Hungarian experiences in an excellent memoir called *The Undefeated*).

A bombed street, Budapest, November 1956. Fortepan.

This time, with brutal efficiency, the uprising was crushed. Hungarian 'patriots', to use the Soviet phrase, had, with Soviet 'assistance', defeated the 'fascist, Hitlerite, counter-revolutionary hooligans' who, financed and encouraged by the 'imperialist west' had tried to seize power from the 'honest, socialist' Hungarians. Just after 1 pm, Moscow radio announced: 'The Hungarian counter-revolution has been crushed'.

Pockets of resistance continued for a few days' longer. Rebels in the town of Stalintown (now called

Dunaújváros) in central Hungary held on until a week later, 11 November.

Over 200,000 Hungarians fled across the border into Austria and the West until that escape route was sealed off.

Post-1956

Up to 3,000 Hungarian civilians had been killed during the uprising, plus 600 Soviet soldiers. 341 Hungarians were executed and 22,000 imprisoned by Janos Kadar's regime in reprisal; many more lost their jobs and their homes, left to face a future of poverty and hunger. The army was thoroughly purged, and the presence of Soviet troops within Hungary increased. AVH men and women killed during the uprising were exhumed and re-buried with full military honours.

On 16 November 1958, the communist Hungarian Working People's Party, now renamed the

Hungarian Socialist Workers' Party, won 99.6 per cent in a single-party election. Everything in Hungary was back to normal.

But the events in Hungary in October – November 1956 had a terrible effect on communist parties in Western Europe. Resigning in disgust, members deserted the communist parties in Great Britain, France and Italy.

Following the return of the Soviet forces on 4 November, Imre Nagy, knowing he was in danger, sought refuge in the Yugoslavian Embassy in Budapest, alongside his wife, daughter, son-in-law and some immediate colleagues, including Pal Maleter, and Julia Rajk. Kadar declared that they were free to leave the embassy without harassment at any time and assured them safe passage out of Hungary. But on 22 November, as they tried to leave the embassy, Nagy and the others were kidnapped by Soviet agents. They were smuggled out of the country and taken to Romania.

Two years' later, Nagy and Maleter were secreted back into Hungary and put on trial. The trial, which lasted from 9 to 15 June 1958, was tape-recorded in its entirety – 52 hours. Charged with high treason and of attempting to overthrow the supposedly legally-recognised Hungarian government, they were found guilty and sentenced to death.

On 16 June 1958, Imre Nagy and Pal Maleter were hanged; their bodies dumped, face down, in unmarked graves. Nagy was 62; Maleter 40. Julia Rajk survived and died, aged 67, in 1981.

Sandor Kopacsi, the chief of Budapest's police who defected to the rebels' cause, was also tried and found guilty. Lucky to escape with his life, he was sentenced to life imprisonment and freed in a 1963 amnesty. He worked in various low-paid manual jobs before emigrating to Canada in 1975, where he died in 2001.

On his release on 28 October, Cardinal Mindszenty lived under voluntary house arrest within Budapest's US embassy and stayed there for fifteen years. When the communists, again worried lest he should die and attain national martyrdom, offered him safe passage to Austria, he refused. Finally, in 1971, on the urging of both Pope Paul VI and US president, Richard Nixon, Mindszenty left Hungary and moved briefly into the Vatican before settling in Vienna.

Cardinal Mindszenty died in Vienna on 6 May 1975, aged 83. He was buried in the city but, following the fall of communism in Hungary, was reinterred in the Hungarian town of Esztergom, where he had been archbishop.

In January 1957, Elvis Presley appeared on the Ed Sullivan Show and sang *Peace in the Valley* in support of the refugees that had fled Hungary. In fact, such was Presley's support for Hungary, raising charitable funds, in 2011 he was named an honourary citizen of Budapest.

Blood in the Water

While the Hungarian Revolution played out, the Hungarian national Olympic water-polo team had been holed up with Russian minders in a hillside hotel in Budapest within earshot of the gun battles raging below.

Hungary was the undoubted superpower of 1950s water polo. They had won gold at three of the four previous Olympic Games, and silver at the London Olympics of 1948; and were firm favourites to triumph again at the Melbourne Olympics of 1956, the first Olympics to be held in the southern hemisphere. The Soviets, jealous of Hungary's success in the water, had been training in Hungary in the months leading up to the Olympics, trying to learn what made the Hungarians so good at their game, thus the Soviet team arrived, uninvited, and made use of Hungary's pool facilities and expertise. A 'friendly' match in Moscow in early 1956 had erupted in violence; the Russians having won thanks to some dubious partisan refereeing.

On 1 November the Olympic team started on their three-week journey to Melbourne not knowing the outcome of the uprising. It was only when they arrived in Australia, they learnt that their oppressive rulers were back in charge. It was at this point that many of the players decided that, once the Olympics were over, they would not be returning to their homeland.

On arriving in the Olympic village in Melbourne, the Hungarian team tore down the Hungarian flag with its central Soviet emblem and replaced it with the traditional Hungarian flag. The Netherlands, Spain and Switzerland boycotted the Games because of the Soviet invasion of Hungary. Egypt, Lebanon and Iraq also boycotted the Games, but over the Suez

Crisis.

The water polo team won their first four games of the tournament against Great Britain, the USA, Italy and Germany. And so they reached the semi-final to face the team that represented their oppressors. The scene was set for a tumultuous confrontation – blood in the water.

The game took place on 6 December. The Hungarian team had decided from the off to conduct a psychological battle by needling their opponents. Having been forced to learn the Russian language two hours a day throughout their school years, the Hungarian players could easily make themselves understood as they mocked their opponents' illegitimacy. Within the first minute of the heavily-charged grudge match, the referee had consigned a Russian player to the sin bin.

Fights continued throughout the game, both above and below the water line. With their method of zonal marking, a revolutionary tactic for the time, the Hungarian team soon had the Soviets ruffled.

The Australian crowd's sympathy clearly lay with the Hungarians, chanting 'Go Hungary' throughout the game and waving the Hungarian flag minus the Soviet emblem. (The Australian team had been beaten by the USSR earlier in the tournament).

With the match drawing to its close, the score was 4-0 to Hungary. In the last couple of minutes, Hungary's star player, the 21-year-old Ervin Zador, was assigned by his captain to mark the Soviet forward, Valentin Prokopov. Zador had already scored two of Hungary's goals. On hearing the referee blow his whistle, Zador made what he called a 'horrible mistake', and momentarily took his eye off the Soviet. He looked back to see Prokopov's arm wind-milling through the air before being thumped a mighty blow that caught him in the eye and cheek. There was, indeed, blood in the water.

The Australian crowd went berserk and surged forward. The police, who had been told to expect trouble, hence their presence at the game, stepped in. The referee blew full time a minute early while the police escorted the Soviet team away from the baying crowd. Ervin Zador was led from the pool with blood pouring from his face. A photograph of the bloodied player has become an iconic image of Cold War-era

Olympics.

Thus, having won, the Hungarian team advanced to the final against Yugoslavia. Zedor, although desperate the play, was unable to – his eye was too swollen. He nervously watched the game from the stands as his teammates triumphed, winning the final 2-1. He received his gold medal on the podium dressed in a suit. (The Soviets won their play-off match, beating Germany 6-4, and hence earned the bronze medal).

The USSR topped the 1956 Olympics' medal table, winning 98 medals (37 gold); the USA came second; Australia third; and Hungary fourth with 26 medals (9 gold). Following the Olympics, Zador, along with half his teammates, sought asylum. It was, he said years later, a difficult decision – he was at the peak of his career and could look forward to a bright sporting future in Hungary. But the Soviet oppression was too much. Thus, he moved to the US and settled in San Francisco. Water polo in the US was not the sport it was in Hungary and, reluctantly, Zedor gave it up. Instead, he took up a job as a swimming instructor and trained a young Mark Spitz, who, at the

Munich Olympics of 1972, won seven gold medals.

2006, the fiftieth anniversary of the Blood in the Water game, saw two cinematic releases based on the event – a documentary, *Freedom's Fury*, executively produced by Quentin Tarantino, no less, and narrated by Zedor's former protégé, Mark Spitz; and an excellent Hungarian feature film, *Children of Glory*.

Ervin Zador died aged 76 on 28 April 2012.

1989

During the 32 years of Janos Kadar's premiership, Hungary prospered as much as a country living under communism can prosper. Collectivization was introduced but this time, the government approached it in a softer manner. More Hungarian children went to school and more school-leavers went to university or took-up places on vocational courses. Standards of living improved, and most families were able to purchase a car – albeit they had no choice of what type of car; the ubiquitous Trabant being the only model within financial reach of all but the party elite. By the late-1960s, Kadar's government could boast that Hungary was the 'the most cheerful barrack in the socialist camp'. People were even allowed to voice their opinions (and criticisms) without fear of reprisal – as long as they didn't take it too far.

It was freedom – of sorts. But 'relative freedom' is still not 'real freedom', and ultimately that is what any individual living in a non-free society aspires to.

Statue of Imre Nagy in the town of Szeged.

Exactly thirty-one years after his execution, on 16 June 1989, Imre Nagy and his colleagues were rehabilitated, reinterred and afforded a public funeral. Six coffins were placed on the steps of the Exhibition Hall in Budapest's Heroes Square. One coffin was empty – representative of all revolutionaries that had fallen in '56.

The ceremony had been organised by a group called the Committee for Historical Justice, set up by former political prisoners and relatives of those who had been executed following the uprising. It was an emotional and symbolic event attended by over 100,000 people. There were no government representatives present. People lined the routes of Budapest and crowded into Heroes' Square, paying their respects to the man who, more than anyone, had symbolised the hope and the ultimate defeat of the uprising. Shops and businesses were closed, schools given the day off. In the square, flowers and wreaths lay everywhere, Corinthian pillars were decked in black and white, Hungarian flags, minus the Soviet emblem, fluttered at half-mast, and Hungarians with bowed heads felt united by grief and ingrained memories. The whole of the country observed a minute's silence. People listened to the eulogies and watched the solemn laying of flowers. They listened to the speeches – words criticising the government and the continued interference of the Soviet Union, and demands for multi-party elections – echoes of 1956; words inconceivable even a few weeks' earlier.

The writing was on the wall for Janos Kadar and Hungary's communist rulers. Sure enough, on the 33rd anniversary of the start of the revolution, 23 October 1989, the People's Republic of Hungary was replaced by the Republic of Hungary with a provisional parliamentary president in place. The road to democracy was swift – parliamentary elections were held in Hungary on 24 March 1990, the first free elections to be held in the country since 1945. The totalitarian government was finished – Hungary, at last, was free.

Meanwhile, on 6 July 1989, the Hungarian judicial acquitted Imre Nagy of high treason. The very same day, Janos Kadar died.

On 7 October 1989, the Hungarian Socialist Workers' Party dissolved itself, no longer wanting to be associated with the 'crimes, mistakes and incorrect ideas and messages' of its Cold War existence.

* * * *

'Hungary conquered and in chains has done more for freedom and justice than any people for twenty years. But for this lesson to get through and convince those in the West who shut their eyes and ears, it was necessary, and it can be no comfort to us, for the people of Hungary to shed so much blood which is already drying in our memories.' Albert Camus.

'The lesson of the Hungarian experience is clear – liberty can be delayed but it cannot be denied. The Soviet Union had crushed the Hungarian uprising but not the Hungarian people's thirst for freedom.' George W. Bush.

'On October 23, 1956, the Hungarian people stood up against tyranny in the name of freedom, bravely rising up to oppose the Communist regime which had been imposed upon them by the Soviet Union. During this uprising, many Hungarians died to defend and advance their country's freedom and independence.' Barack Obama.

'Of course, modern Russia is not the Soviet Union, but we can still feel some sort of moral responsibility for these events. Our task is not to forget the past and to think about the future.'
Vladimir Putin.

The Torn Flag

The Torn Flag is a novel I wrote about the events in Hungary in 1949 and culminating during the uprising of 1956:

Sometimes the simplest of choices can have the most devastating of consequences. Sometimes falling in love can be a curse. Sometimes being the hard man is the hardest job.

Hungary, 1949. George, Eva and Zoltan. Three people trying to live by the rules within a system that demands total obedience.

George, a rising star of Hungarian football, is told to throw a game. Faced with an impossible dilemma, George has to decide – to risk everything to fulfil his dream or, for the sake of his future, obey the rules.

Eva, reeling from tragedy, falls in love at a time when love is fraught with danger.

Zoltan works for the secret police where having a heart is a sign of weakness. A torn man trying to suppress the good within him, his job takes him further and further from the things he values most.

Seven years' later, in 1956, their destinies collide as Hungary erupts into revolution. Secrets can no longer be hidden as loyalties are pushed to the limit.

Set against the violent backdrop of suppression and revolution, 'The Torn Flag' is a tale of people caught in the machinations of history, where the choices you make determine your fate.

Reviews:

"Impactful. Heart-wrenching. An important read."

"Finished The Torn Flag – loved it! Recognised a number of scenes during the Hungarian Revolution – clearly done the research! Thought the female characters were particularly believable and well written. So just wanted to say I enjoyed it!"

"I want to give this to others without [an ebook reader] to read it."

"Emotion bubbles throughout the novel's pages."

"A skilfully developed, suspenseful plot keeps the story moving."

"The characters come alive — you get into their heads. They are empathetic or cruel and heartless, but always interesting. There is the dark side of human nature as well as its opposite."

You can read an extract from *The Torn Flag* on rupertcolley.com/novels/the-torn-flag.

Available as an ebook and paperback from Amazon.

* * * * *

Images

All the images used in this book are, as far as I can ascertain, in the public domain. If I have mistakenly used an image that is not in the public domain, please let me know at rupert@historyinanhour.com and I shall remove / replace the offending item.

Other works by Rupert Colley:

Fiction:

This Time Tomorrow – 'Two brothers. One woman. A nation at war.' Part One of *The Searight Saga*, a compelling story of war, brotherly love, passion and betrayal during World War One. Vast in scope and intimate in the portrayal of three lives swept along by circumstances.

The Unforgiving Sea – 'Ten men adrift on a lifeboat. Only one will live to tell the tale.' Part Two of *The Searight Saga*. On its surface, a tale of murder, survival and loss set in World War Two, while at its core we find a story of deep love, loyalty and forgiveness.

The Woman on the Train – 'Someone saves your life. How far will you go to repay the debt?' A wartime debt threatens to ruin a musician's career and much more.

The White Venus – 'When the ties of loyalty are severed, whom do you trust?' Set in Nazi-occupied France during World War Two, a coming-of-age tale of divided loyalties, trust and a tragedy never forgotten but never mentioned.

The Black Maria – 'When love becomes your greatest enemy.' A love story set in 1930s Soviet Union, a novel about fear: fear of each other, fear of being denounced, fear of Stalin's secret police; and, ultimately, the fear of falling in love.

My Brother the Enemy – 'Fear on the streets. Death on every corner. But the real enemy is the brother at his side.' A story of jealousy, sibling rivalry and betrayal, and a desperate bid for freedom, set against the backdrop of Nazi oppression and war.

The Torn Flag – 'Sometimes the simplest of choices can have the most devastating of consequences.' Set during the Hungarian Revolution, an epic tale of people caught in the machinations of history, where the choices you make determine your fate.

The Sixth Man – 'Six prisoners. Five must die. Who will live?' 1944. A Nazi prison in France. Six French prisoners; five face execution. They have one night to decide who should live and who should die.

Non-fiction:

The 'History In An Hour' series
Published by HarperCollins.

The Savage Years: Tales From the 20th Century, a collection of sixty essays covering the two world wars, the Soviet Union, Nazi Germany, the Cold War, black history and much more.

The Battle of the Somme

A History of the World Cup

Historyinanhour.com

Rupertcolley.com